The
Crowd-Sourced
MARRIAGE

The Crowd-Sourced MARRIAGE

Leveraging Your Trusted Community to Help You Marry Well

SHARLA BICKLEY LANGSTON

TATE PUBLISHING
AND **ENTERPRISES**, LLC

Published by Tate Publishing & Enterprises, LLC
127 E. Trade Center Terrace | Mustang, Oklahoma 73064 USA
1.888.361.9473 | www.tatepublishing.com

Tate Publishing is committed to excellence in the publishing industry. The company reflects the philosophy established by the founders, based on Psalm 68:11,
"The Lord gave the word and great was the company of those who published it."

Book design copyright © 2014 by Tate Publishing, LLC. All rights reserved.
Cover design by Jim Villaflores
Interior design by Jake Muelle

Published in the United States of America

ISBN: 978-1-63268-075-4
Religion / Christian Life / Love & Marriage
14.07.11

To my Mom, Raye Bickley, who prayed for Mr. Sharla all those years (I'll send your copy to heaven) and to the singles with a deep longing to be part of something bigger through the commitment of marriage.

ACKNOWLEDGMENTS

Thanks to Jesus for giving His life for me and you so we could experience life abundantly.

Thanks to the community of believers at Highland Park Presbyterian Church in Dallas, Texas, who shepherded me for a decade and modeled Christ's love.

Thanks to the community of believers at Northwest Bible Church in Dallas, Texas, for pouring into Mark, strengthening his faith, and preparing a place where we can live out our marriage desperately dependent on Jesus.

And thanks to my hubby, Mark, who's beyond my hopes and dreams for a man after God's heart.

CONTENTS

Appendix

PREFACE

When it comes to meeting people to date, singles have plenty of options. A recent study published in the journal *Proceedings of the National Academy of Sciences* and funded by eHarmony examined the marital status and satisfaction of 19,131 people who tied the knot between 2005 and 2012. This research suggests that one in three Americans now meet their spouses online and that those marriages are more satisfying and less likely to end in divorce than those that begin by more traditional means.

As popular and acceptable as online dating has become, this book heads in the opposite direction. Maybe the idea of arranged marriages had some value we can apply today. The idea is that those closest to you, including your family, friends, and community of faith, bring wisdom and shared values into the picture. Why not tap into the depth and breadth of love from the people you hold most dear and who have your best at heart? *The Crowd-Sourced Marriage* follows one woman's journey to embrace her community while searching for God's best in a mate.

WHY THIS BOOK?

I read it somewhere, probably on Pinterest: "Do more of what makes you Happy Holy." I believe that life as a couple is more than 1+1=2, and that trusting the Lord and the people with whom He has surrounded you can work to make your life brighter and more holy. I'm living proof of God's faithfulness, and I want the same for you. May this book equip you for the journey and encourage you to laugh at yourself and at circumstances along the way. Enjoy the ride.

"For the Lord is good; his steadfast love endures forever, and his faithfulness continues through all generations." (Psalm 100:5, ESV).

INTRODUCTION

My dating career spans more than three decades, which is more than thirty consecutive years, ages sixteen to forty-eight. In most professions, thirty-plus years of experience usually brings expertise. I met my husband at age forty-eight and tied the knot five weeks after my fiftieth birthday. In those thirty-plus years of dating, I never came close to being engaged. I did have one marriage proposal at forty-eight from a 104-year-old man at church who followed the proposal with the statement, "I think we could have a beautiful life together." I was not interested in marrying this sweet gentleman, but I hoped for his attitude and tenacity in my later years.

Growing up the fourth of three wanted children to parents with eighteen siblings for Dad and nine siblings for Mom, I knew no other lifestyle than marriage and kids. Surely I would graduate college, work a year or two, marry, have kids, and live the life our society considers the norm. Not so, and as with Ruth in the Bible, I moved into Plan B. This book celebrates the journey of being single and God's plan and timing for my life.

My biggest hope for you and your friends is encouragement as you pursue the dream of finding God's best in a mate. Although your timeline may not mirror mine, please know it is God's timing that works best. Allow the journey to help build trust in the God who pursues you and who gave His son so that you may have abundant life.

"May the God of hope fill you with all joy and peace as you trust in him, so that you may overflow with hope by the power of the Holy Spirit" (Romans 15:13, NIV).

A LITTLE HISTORY

Before sharing the crowd-sourcing approach to dating, let me tell you a little background on this Louisiana girl. I was born in England to a US Air Force family and made my way to the States at the ripe old age of eighteen months. Hence, I do not have a sexy British accent to win the attention of boys. I dated very little at Parkway High School in Bossier City. My first date was in my junior year to a party with a cute senior boy. I was not a party girl, and he drank so much that I ended up driving us home while he barfed out the car window. I left him in the car in his driveway and walked home. What a stellar start to a dating career.

Thankfully, I was surrounded with twelve awesome girlfriends who, to this day, share their lives with me. We recently gathered at the lake home of one of them and reflected on how God has worked in each of our lives over the years to keep us together, bring us to faith in Jesus Christ, and laugh right along with us. The PHS Chicks know my heart and soul and cheered me along all those single years, and I love them mightily.

After high school, I followed my two older brothers off to Louisiana State University—Geaux Tigers!—and into the same academic major in Petroleum Engineering. Someone told me the geology classes were 95 percent guys, and they were right. In spite of these good odds, I left college with a B.S. not a *Mrs.*

For the next eight years, I followed the oil company career path working for four years in the Gulf of Mexico where there were plenty of guys, but not many with teeth. Then I experienced four years in Alaska where it is said, "The odds are good, but the goods are odd." I can testify that statement to be true. My favorite singles advertisement asked, "send picture of boat and motor." I learned to fish, ski, mountain bike, and backpack. I dated a really nice guy for a few years, and once we discussed marriage in a third-person perspective, but that was as close as I came to marrying.

My parents' dating and marriage story went like this: three dates in three days and he asked her to marry him and have three kids. Hence, I'm the fourth of three wanted children. I used to joke with my mom occasionally by calling her on a Wednesday saying I met a great boy on Saturday and we were going to marry. She would kindly caution me that life was so different back in the day she married and to take more time to really get to know him. Once in my early thirties, I called to play the "I'm going to marry the guy I met on Saturday" game, and she just responded with an "Okay." Game over.

For years, I attributed the deep emptiness inside me to the lack of love for and with a man. I dated some and had a few serious relationships, but none headed toward marriage.

The emptiness continued. In 1992, I took a severance package, left Alaska, and traveled the world. I was in search of adventure and thought that exploring different cultures and people would fill the hole in my soul. It was a blast traipsing across the outback of Australia, into Central and South America, through Greece, Turkey, Eastern Europe, and the Nordic countries. The more I saw, the more I wanted to see. The time away didn't satisfy my hunger for adventure, but instead fed the desire to keep exploring.

After eleven months, I moved to Washington, D.C. to work on Capitol Hill where sausage is made. The next four years were exciting but empty of personal purpose and meaning. My sweet friends Christy and Peggy could see my hollow soul. I was in an emotional "ditch" involving breaking up with a guy I thought I'd marry. Through my friends' love and care and the ministry of the Christian Embassy, God became front and center in my life. My coming to faith in Jesus revolved around control. Figuring out I was not in control brought a huge wave of relief to my life, and I no longer felt alone on this journey. I could look back and see God's hand and timing in my life. I am so grateful I did not marry before understanding who God is and His call in my life. Without His intervention, I might have ended up unequally yoked and struggling in a marriage mismatch.

I left D.C. with Jesus in my heart, and a longing to see Africa. I flew into Cape Town and spent two months on safari photographing the Big Five in South Africa, Zambia,

19

Zimbabwe, Botswana, and Kenya. For most folks, the Big Five safari animals are the leopard, lion, cape buffalo, elephant, and rhinoceros, but I managed to expand to the Big Six, which included a handsome British Army officer. Most of this trip was on my own, but for a few weeks a friend met me for the adventure. It was during a site-seeing tour of Kenya that our van went a little too deep in the mud. Shortly after getting stuck, the handsome British Army officer appeared in a jeep and offered to take us to the next village, while the tour guide worked on the situation. We enjoyed a cold cola together and soon enough our van appeared. Best Safari Ever!

Back in the States, I moved to Dallas to work in the oil industry again. This time, I was learning about drilling wells in west Texas and South America. I spent fourteen to twenty-eight days at a time living on a drilling rig as the only female. In the oil and gas industry, major companies contract with drilling rig companies such that there are usually two to three oil company employees, and the rest are contractors for drilling or other service companies. The hierarchy puts the oil company employees over the contractors. So, not only was I the only female, but effectively had seventy-five guys working for me. One particularly hot and humid day in the Andean jungle, I decided to walk around the operations areas, practice my pitiful Spanish, and learn new skills. I commented to one Peruvian guy after another how hot it was by fanning my face and exclaiming,

"Caliente, Caliente!" Most of these guys had never seen a Caucasian woman and hadn't laid eyes on any female in over two months. My attempt to make small talk about the oppressive weather translated to how "hot-to-trot" I was. That went over famously. I didn't get a date out of the deal but heard a lot of offers for "Cerveza y Lima." My dating challenges continued, even across international borders.

I took my first mission trip to Kenya when I was thirty-eight years old. One of our teammates was a vibrant, interesting woman in her mid-seventies. She had married at age fifty for the first time and had lived an amazing and fulfilled life. Marrying at fifty seemed like a horrible nightmare, and all I could do was beg God not to wait until I was fifty to bring the man of my dreams into my life. Ha! This was yet another timing lesson God had for me: Beg all you want, but God is going to do what is best for you.

The oil field proved to be a difficult lifestyle. I was away from Dallas more than half the time and utterly exhausted when at home. After a few years, Mobil and Exxon merged, and I opted out. God was gracious, and a position at my home church, Highland Park Presbyterian, opened up leading the Christian Service ministry. I jumped at the opportunity, took a 75 percent pay cut, traded the BMW for a Honda, and moved in to a house with two roommates. God can do 180s better than anyone, and I was able to trade in drilling for oil for drilling for *souls*. The change was a relief in so many ways, yet challenging in ways I had never dreamed. Yes, the church is full of sinners, me included, and in spite of it all, we are loved deeply by a forgiving God. My new role as church mouse had plenty of benefits, but none better than the lessons of true Christian community. Church staff and members became my family. They shared their lives, their kids, and their hearts with me, and I learned so much about God's love through them. I was still lonely, but it was different, as God used so many folks to give me an abundant single life. My friend and roommate, Catharine, loved me enough to teach me about conflict. In a house with three women this was a needed skill. Here I was thirty-six years old and moving backward in the typical trajectory of life. Most my friends were rooming with their husbands and I was giving up my independent living to share with two roomies. God knew I needed some unwinding from my selfish ways and sharing living space was His way of showing me love. It was hard, yet in the end, I value the time I spent learning to share my life and valuing the needs of others.

Life moseyed along. For the longest time I thought I'd marry a man and his house, but at some point I ditched this long-term expectation and, at forty, took the real estate plunge. I learned a lot while owning a home on a church mouse salary, especially why it would be beneficial to have a hubby. I was blessed with many wonderful roommates whose sole purpose was to keep me out of the neatnik rut I dug. It was a stretch to share a bathroom in my own home, but one I prayed God would honor one day when I shared a bathroom with a husband.

I loved my work helping others discover their spiritual gifts and find a fit in the ministry. I was able to venture on a mission trip each year and served through a few local ministries. My knowledge and trust of the Lord increased, yet the desire for a hubby and the pain in loneliness did not disappear. Still, intimacy with Christ deepened to levels I had not understood before. I had my moments and seasons of overwhelming sadness. It is difficult to understand or describe sorrow when the object of grief is intangible. Did I want children? Yes, but for me there was an order to that dream. *I am an engineer, you know.* I count it a true blessing that I did not suffer the desire for children outside of being married to a man I loved. Over the years, I have met plenty of single women and men with deep yearnings for their own children. I cannot begin to understand their pain. As my body clock ticked away, I felt a distant and dull ache as I reached and passed forty, grieving what I never experienced.

God revealed Himself in other ways, and I found myself experiencing several life-giving groups of people who had life-changing impacts on me. The first was the young family of Jeff and Ellen Schulz, both associate pastors at my church. They had two small boys that brought me great joy and laughter. Jeff and Ellen invested deeply in me. They lived out the Christian life with me at the dinner table, the gym, at work, at the kids' sporting events, and in the monotony of daily chores. By the time boys number three and four had arrived, I felt like the luckiest aunt alive. The Schulz family celebrated as life happened, not just birthdays and the other usual holidays. When the second-born, Emerson, became potty trained, Ellen invited the neighbors over for an impromptu celebration. I had never been to a potty party, and not knowing what to bring, showed up with pictures of toilets from around the world hoping it would inspire Emerson in some way. He is an inspiring young man now, but I don't think it was the multicultural potties that did it.

The second group was the small group Bible study of godly and fun women, with whom I experienced life-on-life. Christine, Elizabeth, Kelly, Linda, and Mary Lee are precious sisters in Christ who, to this day, know my soul from its dark depths to its sparkling heights. In the early years, we were all single and shared daily conversations, activities, joys, and tears. Over time, they each married, moved, and started families. No words can explain the gift each of these women is to me, and no small group will ever compare. Our Facebook group is called "The BEST small group ever," and we continue to pray and share our lives—struggles and dreams alike.

I am convinced God used these two experiences to shape me and sharpen me for marriage. Living authentically with others multiplies the blessings and helps softens the blows. I am both encouraged and challenged by God's instruction in the Book of James:

Real wisdom, God's wisdom, begins with a holy life and is characterized by getting along with others. It is gentle and reasonable, overflowing with mercy and blessings, not hot one day and cold the next, not two-faced. You can develop a healthy, robust community that lives right with God and enjoy its results *only* if you do the hard work of getting along with each other, treating each other with dignity and honor.

James 3:17–18 (MSG)

I pray there are folks in your life loving you and blessing your path with Jesus. True Christian community doesn't compare with any other people group in terms of its value in preparing you for heaven.

DATING 101

In 2007, I read a great book by Henry Cloud, *How to Get a Date Worth Keeping*. It was inspirational and overwhelming as Dr. Cloud challenged singles to find or create five interactions a week with:

1. Someone (a guy, in my case) not previously known to you;

2. Interact long enough to generate interest; and

3. Create some way for him to know how to contact you.

At the time I read the book, I didn't have five interactions a year! Dr. Cloud teaches singles to open up their small box of lists and requirements for a mate and date a variety of types. His reasoning is that you never know whom you might meet while out with a new person, and that by dating lots of different folks, you could figure out a few things you would like and dislike in a mate. I encourage you to read the book and learn from Dr. Cloud's guidance.

How to Get a Date Worth Keeping challenged me to take action. Heck, I had tried the traditional routes: mutual friends, online dating, blind dates, double dates, clubs (both bars and mutual interest types), so why not something new? I started Team Sharla, a crowd of friends to come alongside me in my desire to meet, date, and marry a godly man. Think of it as *crowd-sourcing* for dating. Knowing this new approach might necessitate additional financial resources, I took steps to enhance the miniscule discretionary spending line item in my church mouse budget. I contacted my financial planner, Doug, a long-time friend from college, and tapped into my savings for a little "social money." I also found plenty of free stuff to do around town. An outing to Lowe's or Home Depot proved to be a great way to pursue the encounters described in the challenge listed above.

One evening, Laura and Charles, a wonderful couple and dear friends, invited me along on their family dinner outing with their sixteen-year-old Chas. As dinner concluded, I explained I would be darting off Home Depot because I only had four of my five interactions for the week. Chas seemed amused, but the poor guy is probably scarred for life thinking women are stalking the isles of big box hardware stores to meet guys in order to get their numbers up.

The year 2007 did not prove to be the year for me to change my single status, but I had a blast. I pursued new interests, interacted with new people in brand new ways, and made some new friends that, to this day, are some of my favorite people. Thanks, Jim and Brad! Just because the outcome wasn't what I hoped, the process itself was redeeming. And isn't that the case with so much of life? It isn't so much about the destination as it is the journey that takes you there. Enjoy your singlehood to the maximum and leave the outcome to God.

WHY A TEAM?

The idea behind crowd-sourcing, is forming a team. Why a team? I'm not a sports nut—just ask my stepdaughter Jackie, who's Miss Football, and stepson Spencer, who's Mr. Baseball. According to Wikipedia, a team "comprises a group of people or animals linked in a common purpose. Teams are especially appropriate for conducting tasks that are high in complexity and have many interdependent subtasks." I especially like the part about having animals on the team.

Allow me to digress here. During Team Sharla, I had two cats and two dogs. Atticus is an orange tabby with a sweet spot for catching prey and bringing it home for me, still alive and kickin'. He is a good example of what a man in my life could be—a champ at rat-killing and removing pests from my presence. Then there's Harley Hank, another orange tabby and a mean purring machine, hence the name Harley. Harley Hank is charming and loving, which are also great qualities for my man. And then came Zeke, the *dude*! He exemplifies why humans love dogs: adoring, playful, and enjoys running alongside me when I donned my inline skates. What woman wouldn't want Zeke's qualities in a man? Number four, and the only animal to make it into the marriage contract, is Zoe, a rescued Australian cattle dog, part chicken and part kangaroo. She must have had suffered abuse by a male, as she is afraid of *all* of them. My hubby is the only man she trusts, which gives me some comfort on a weird level.

But a woman cannot live on Wikipedia and pets alone. God hath provided His Word as guidance for the journey. In Romans 12, Paul uses the analogy of the Body of Christ's believers to the human body.

> In this way we are like the various parts of a human body. Each part gets its meaning from the body as a whole, not the other way around. The body we're talking about is Christ's body of chosen people. Each of us finds our meaning and function as a part of his body. But as a chopped-off finger or cut-off toe we wouldn't amount to much, would we? So since we find ourselves fashioned into all these excellently formed and marvelously functioning parts in Christ's body, let's just go ahead and be what we were made to be, without enviously or pridefully comparing ourselves with each other, or trying to be something we aren't.
>
> Romans 12:4–6 (MSG)

Members of the Body of Christ are uniquely gifted to serve and build the Kingdom. Just as God equips the Body, He gives us community with whom to live out our lives. Alone, we do not possess the knowledge, opportunities, relationships, or creative ideas of a larger group. But as part of a team, our chances of finding God's best improve dramatically. As we live authentically with others, we learn to trust and include them as we pursue our dreams and desires.

God created our bodies with the trust hormone, oxytocin. This brain chemical is stimulated through touch and other warm, welcoming activities such as gazing at one you adore, and maybe even just thinking about them. Some scientists are now seeing oxytocin as the chemical that would help us overcome social apprehension. Can you spell *d-a-t-i-n-g*? God was way ahead of these scientists, so get out there knowing the Lord is on your team. And before you go, pet your critter, hug your roommate, and envision your entire team cheering you on.

BLOG: BIG LOAD OF GARBAGE

This chapter contains the blog entries that served as Team updates from the invitation to participate on the team to the "game over" announcement. The Team timeline was as follows:

> 1/19/10—Team identified and invited
> 2/17/10—First Team update on meeting Mr. Sharla
> 5/19/10—Team on half time
> 4/25/11—Team over, engaged to Mr. Sharla
> 10/13/11—Team celebration, married Mr. Sharla

Again, only God knows your timeline. Your job is to jump in the game. I encourage you to track your progress, journal or, at least, share the high and low points with your Team. In the back of this book are several tools to help you organize your thoughts, talk to the Lord, vent frustrations, or report to the Team. Appendices A–D are a prayer log, team roster, exposure/activity log, and journal pages. Get to work.

YOU'RE DRAFTED

Hi, Team, and Happy New Year. I don't set resolutions, but somehow the timing of this idea seems to fit with the start of a new year. Or maybe it's because the highlights of 2009 included a marriage proposal from a 104-year-old gentleman followed by a date with an ex-gay guy. I don't know the technical term for negative motivation, but I did experience it and decided it was time to create Team Sharla, a version of *crowd-sourcing*. I'm ready to get out of a rut and get serious about finding a date. In 2007, I was intentional about spending time-out and about and experienced an incredible social life. I even met a possible 2010 team member/now great friend, Brad, through the 2007 effort. What a bonus.

It's time to resurrect the old team and enhance it with new friends and ideas. The major takeaways from Dr. Henry Cloud's book, *How to Get a Date Worth Keeping*, are 1) My job is prayer and attitude, and 2) Your job is prayer and exposure. You are receiving this e-mail because I love and respect you, and your friendship means a great deal to me. So what do you think? Will you be on the team? For those of you who served before, I hope it was an enjoyable experience. Put on that Team Sharla visor and head out to Home Depot, your favorite patio bar, a Habitat for Humanity build, the gym, or wherever life takes you *and me*.

For those of you who have no clue what I am talking about, consider yourself drafted into the army it will take to get me a date! Some of you have specific skills that I do not possess. Like Brad, Michael, Todd, Robin…well, you are guys, and I am not. Your input starts merely by its viewpoint. Lisa—photography skills for those online dating applications; Krissy—well, you know, the fashion and flirting thing. For the rest of you, I am up for any type of social outing or idea whatsoever. It's all about exposure, baby. So consider me your third wheel to a party, escort to an event, sucker to try a new hot spot, guinea pig on any outing. For you, out of state friends, sure, I am up for an out-of-town date, but more importantly, I'm just hoping you will be on the team in heart and in prayer. If you need a visor, let me know. If you possess marketing/ merchandising skills, let me know and we can come up with something new. If you are a techie with web page design experience, step on up!

For those of you with spouses whom I know feel free to share the burden/spirit with them. I didn't intentionally leave them off the e-mail, just didn't get complete coverage.

Just so you know—we cannot fail. I have a date tonight and a setup on Wednesday, so 2010 goals are already met. It is icing on the cake moving forward. Don't you love overachievers? Who would have thought the Martin Luther King holiday could be so productive?

Love,
S+

COACHING NOTES: INVITATION IDEAS

Everyone loves an invitation, so put some thought into it. Have formal invites printed, or record a song or poem of invite. Use your creativity, and if you don't have any, borrow some. Pinterest is waiting.

COACHING NOTES: WHO'S YOUR TEAM?

As for team members, I suggest you invite family, friends, neighbors, coworkers, church buddies, your favorite Starbuck barista, the postal person...whatever it takes to get your dream top of mind with as many trusted folks as you can. Turn now to the back section in the book entitled "Team Roster," and jot down as many folks as you can to think of. You can add more later and there is no limit.

THE GOODS

Humans are capable of amazing feats for cheap, worldly trinkets. Ever spent $27 at the state fair shooting water into a clown's mouth for a stuffed toy? Ever groveled on the streets of New Orleans for a few plastic Mardi Gras beads?

Well, no team is complete without team memorabilia. Stickers and visors were a hit in 2007, but 2010 deserves an update. If I were a real techie, I'd invent some app to help remind you about the team purpose and ideas for the game. This blog hits the limits of my geek skills, so it is back to the cheap carnival idea bin. Be checking your mail/ doorstep for your new treasures. If your creative juices gurgle in this area, please let me know. Thank you, Elizabeth, for the koozie/drink holder idea!

Love,
S+

COACHING NOTES: TEAM GOODS

It's time to invest in your team. There are thousands of great products you can personalize to incentivize your team and advertise your platform. I've created a link on my website to a great place for ordering your Team Goods. Go to SharlaLangston.com. Once you receive your goods, make distribution an official team activity (maybe a happy hour or team biking event).

For 2010, Team Sharla received coffee cup koozies (it was January after all) with "Team Sharla—I'm on the Team" emblazoned on the side, and team members were reminded with every sip of their eight-dollar latte of the most important mission of the day: "pray and get me a date."

Team Goods are practical, everyday items that your team members will use frequently and while out in public. For example, my two dear friends, D'Ann and Terese, have breakfasted with me weekly for the past ten years. We share our lives, struggles, and joys. We also share September as our birthday month, so we decided to join a Habitat for Humanity community build to celebrate together. They looked so great in Team Sharla visors! Now, that is team spirit.

Team Goods—coffee koozie

OUTING #1

There we were, me and team member Kitty, sitting at the bar in Houston's minding our own business, when he sat down. He didn't look like a criminal, so when he started chatting, I remembered the newly adopted open attitude and enjoyed the conversation. He was quite the foodie and spoke of his favorites all about town. We even shared Avila's as our favorite Mexican food restaurant. As I thought it to be harmless enough, I agreed to meet for the *best burger in Texas* at The Grape a few days later.

Sure enough, he was there, same UT ball cap and all. And it was quite nice. Not deep. Just light and interesting—what first dates are supposed to be. It was only after finishing the first half of the *best burger in Texas* that I was nosy enough to ask for his last name. I can't remember it. I do not have his phone number or e-mail. Perfect.

Love,
S+

COACHING NOTES: READY, SET, GO

Once your Team is in action, you *will* get asked out on a date. So put on that good attitude and say yes. I stuck to my rule that I would go out with anything but a hardened criminal. I figured reformed criminals should remain candidate material since they had plenty to talk about from their therapy and life-change experience. You know your limits, but let me offer this: you are not going to marry this guy on this date. So he doesn't have to be a Christian, tall enough, well-dressed, or have all his hair. You are just going on a date to understand more about interacting with the opposite sex and learning about another human being. Now, get out there.

OUTING #2

My friend Gabby decided I should meet her friend Bruce. The plan was 7 p.m. at the bar at Gloria's. I arrived at seven, looked around the bar, saw no Gabby, and ordered a margarita. A moment later, a guy about the height and hair color of Bruce as described by Gabby walked toward me. I politely asked, "Are you Bruce?" He leaned in toward me to repeat the question and responded in a low, slimy voice, "Do I need to be?" Not as politely, I answered, "No."

I moved to the next chair. He stood by and ordered a drink. Then he decided he was Bruce and explained that he was just playing around. I responded that it was a good thing he was joking because the slime was thick on the initial interaction. He continued to check out everyone else at the bar, made a few more slimy comments, and then turned halfway around to stare into the restaurant. A few moments passed before he slid off to the other side of the bar. Odd, very odd.

I texted Gabby to please not be alarmed, but I would be leaving soon after a polite hello to her and her husband. Gabby phoned from a table in the restaurant trying to find me. As it turned out, the real Bruce was just joining them. Things got a lot better. The real Bruce gained a few points merely by not being the *slime* Bruce.

Our dinner was quite pleasant. Bruce had a dog named Zoe, so he scored a few more points.

Love,
S+

COACHING NOTES: PERSEVERANCE

At times, I felt the Team was getting more out of this than I was. Slimy Bruce was one of those times. I am pretty sure Paul did not write Romans 5:3 with Bruce in mind, "Not only so, but we also glory in our sufferings, because we know that suffering produces perseverance…" But I do know you can't give up after your first Bruce experience. It's early in the game and you are strengthening your resolve, and the suffering is worth it.

OUTING #3

In true team fashion, Carl was in Cuba, so I got to be Margaret's date to UAFF Kid Film Festival party. The art scene was way out of my normal circles, but it was a fun event. Nothing to report.

We decided to stop at Houston's on the way home. Upon arrival, an eighty-seven-year-old Irish guy took to us immediately. He checked out Margaret's left ring finger and moved on to me. Margaret had to be one of the kindest souls on the planet and engaged him in a very dear conversation about the state of his widowerhood.

Upon leaving, the guy a few stools down decided to chat with us. He was harmless enough. Team mentality said to take every offer, so we dallied a bit before leaving him my number and toodling on home. Can you believe I left my number on a cocktail napkin? So 1980s.

Love,
S+

COACHING NOTES: FLEXIBILITY

You've got to keep your plans flexible. If the first outing doesn't produce, create another. If the first guy that talks to you doesn't have his real teeth, just wait until the next guy.

E-DATING

I'd prefer an arranged marriage to dating online with eHarmony.com, match.com, plentyofish.com, and chemistry.com. Yuck. But the team deserves a good laugh every once in a while, so I am on them all.

A few years ago on eHarmony, I was matched with a guy, muddled through all the steps of preferences, questions and answers, then to e-mail and finally a telephone conversation. It was my first time to talk with him and he divulges his desire to have six kids. He was forty-eight! Why I agreed to meet for dinner, I do not know other than Team loyalty. But I did get to hear all about his brain surgery the prior year and view his really neat scar. The next week, my friend Valerie was matched with him too. He expressed his desire for six kids to her as well. What fun we had e-mailing him together and telling him that between the two of us, maybe we could satisfy the half dozen desire. It freaked him out. Sure was fun.

Love,
S+

COACHING NOTES: VIRTUAL MADNESS

You gotta do it—online dating is the reward your team gets for wearing the silly visor. I have done my share of online dating over the years. One of the nicest friends I ever made came through eHarmony. Jim is a cute, normal, Christian guy, and I am thankful for the years of friendship we enjoyed without being in a dating relationship. Early on, my friends tagged him with the name "Crockpot" because they thought he was moving so slowly. Jim was just good at being friends, and there is nothing wrong with that.

On a different note, did you know Craigslist has a singles section? I thought it was just for selling your junk and buying other people's junk. I was searching for some item one day and saw the Personals section for the first time. I clicked on it and soon spotted a guy with an LSU ball cap, Geaux Tigers. Now, that's just pure Craigslist treasure. The *Tiger* and I exchanged a few e-mails and were planning to meet in person later in the week.

On Thursday night, a windstorm knocked a huge limb out of the tree and onto my back deck. On Friday, my multitasking nature took over as I decided to blend sawing the tree limb with having friends over and inviting the *Tiger* to join us. I figured it was a safe way to get to know someone in a crowd of my own peeps. At the beginning of the chainsaw/margarita party, as it is now known, *Tiger* seemed pretty normal. My friend Elaine is a hardcore, yet good, interviewer. She was drilling him with questions, and we found out the scoop on this guy, including the details of his wife's cheating escapades. He then told the story of mowing his yard one afternoon, pausing to rest on the tailgate of his pickup truck and witnessing a car hitting a squirrel in the street right in front of his house. He actually admitted, proud even, of scraping it off the road, skinning it, and making a "darn good squirrel gumbo." No lie.

My dear friend and neighbor of ten years, Lisa, listened to this story with her jaw dropped open. Lisa was from Ohio, and I guess they don't scrape and skin road kill for gumbo up there. She hounded me on that story for some time. Lisa passed away from breast cancer in 2012 and is missed dearly by her friends and family. I know she is still laughing about *Tiger*, right along with that squirrel. Note to self: Leave Craigslist to buying and selling junk.

FROZEN

Hey, Team,

So little activity this week, I thought I'd fill the blog time by changing the scenery/background design on the blog page. Frozen.

Hey, Team, this weekend is Superbowl—need a Team Sharla event to attend!

Love,

S+

COACHING NOTES: THE OFF-SEASON

Yes, there will be gaps in action. That is why Pinterest exists. Keep yourself sharp during the drought by pretending your pets are new to you. Chat with them. No, wait, don't do this. Just be patient, drink lots of water, and know your time on the bench will end soon.

MARCH MADNESS

Wow, what a spectacular month!

Ball Cap Guy is still around. We had dinner at Houston's—no surprise—but in the dining room where you can't wear a ball cap. He has hair. Not much, but some. It was a mystery uncovered. We had dinner at The Grape—again, no surprise there.

Sad news. Today, Terrilli's Restaurant burned down. Terrilli's is Ball Cap Guy's Sunday brunch spot. Hope he makes it to Monday. So this Sunday, it is a movie and dinner, and with Avila's closed and Terrilli's burned down, what new place might we discover?

Love,
S+

COACHING NOTES: THROW IN THE TOWEL

I should have stopped going out with Ball Cap Guy a few dates back, but something in my engineering background and general personality type insisted I finish things, even if they didn't appear to merit finishing. Ball Cap Guy was not a Christian, although we chatted about faith frequently. I made no secret of my faith, and he was happy as a post-believer. Listen to your heart after you have given someone else a chance to reveal themselves, and when the time is right, move on. You can only eat at the same three restaurants so many times before it gets boring.

LOVE THY NEIGHBOR

Hi, Team,

So have I told you about my friend and neighbor Curry? What an awesome chica.

Curry introduced me to a friend of hers from Northwest Bible Church, and we'll call him Nice Fella, because he is.

NICE FELLA

We've had coffee on a Friday, lunch the next Friday, and dinner scheduled for this Friday. Maybe he gave up dating for Lent and fishes on Fridays.

Nice Fella is a gem. He is an entrepreneur, high energy, relational, involved in great ministry stuff.

Love,

S+

COACHING NOTES:
A TALE OF LOVE AND REDEMPTION

If your past is marred by mistakes and sin, join the crowd. I see myself as a tarnished saint, someone purified and shiny new at the core by Jesus's sacrifice, yet discolored and sullied by life lived in this world. I have seen God's redemptive work in the lives of so many, including myself, and have a story to encourage you with His goodness and love.

Curry and Joe had been married for eight years when they moved into the house next door to me in April of 2009. By August, Joe had moved out, and in January 2010, they divorced. Curry allowed me to walk with her in this hardship of faith. I learned so much from this tarnished saint and continue to enjoy her friendship and mentorship. In February 2010, the Lord did a miraculous and prayed-for work in Joe's heart as he accepted Christ as Savior. This was the same month I met Mark.

Our paths as couples paralleled each other in a strange, yet familiar way. Curry and Joe started to *date* again as Mark and I started our relationship. Curry was dating a new man, as was I. The abbreviated version of our paths is that Curry and Joe remarried two weeks before Mark and I married. Now, we have a new friendship as couples and are blessed by the redemptive work God continues to do in all of our lives. Please don't let your past diminish your hope for the future. God can handle it if you will just hand it over to Him.

JUNIOR HIGH

Last night while on the phone with Nice Fella, a text came through from Ball Cap Guy. I haven't seen this much action since seventh grade—maybe not even then.

Love,

S+

50

COACHING NOTES: ACTION

I do not have a rich dating history in terms of action. In college, my dorm suitemates were preparing for my second-year-anniversary-without-a-date party when I stumbled into a relationship with the guy who became my college boyfriend. Don't give up during the dry spells. Find some way to celebrate them. You have a team that would help you!

AND THE BEAT GOES ON

This weekend marked the first time in my life to go out with three guys in twenty-four hours: Saturday night with Nice Fella, Sunday lunch with Crockpot (I don't know if that really counts as a date, but what the heck), and Sunday night with Ball Cap Guy. All the while, I was suffering from whatever new fungus that blew in from West Texas. They make drugs for times like these.

Love,
S+

COACHING NOTES: ENJOY THE FRENZY

As mentioned before, I do multitask well—and often. But this skill did not lend itself to the increased dating activity I experienced. Expect to learn about yourself in this Team approach. It doesn't mean you have to like it; I didn't. I learned I am a one-horse-cart kind of girl, and God's design for monogamy suits me to a tee.

NOTHING NEW

There were no new additions to speak of, but ongoing activity with Nice Fella is very enjoyable. We had a nice walk with our dogs last Saturday and had plans to go to the Dallas Stars hockey game on Tuesday night.

Love,
S+

COACHING NOTES: AGING WELL

There is something to be said for getting older. Maybe it was the encouragement from Dr. Cloud's book to relax and enjoy the date and not worry about the future. Maybe maturity caught up with me, or just maybe it was because Nice Fella was the One for me. Getting to know him was the easiest dating experience ever. I was enjoying the small things, the conversations, and becoming good friends. It felt right, and I was happy being with him without wondering what was next. Praise God.

E-DATING (CONTINUED)

Can I tell you what an adventure it is to date online? Here is a recent sampling of those who have "winked" at me, "viewed" me, or "matched" with me:

- 31-year-old director of a fashion and design college library and whose favorite place is CiCi's

- 5'7" tall and whose favorites include *The Oprah Winfrey Show*

- 32 of them enjoy "walks on the beach at sunset"

- 12 enjoy candlelight dinners

- 7 have a thing for "snuggling"

- 89% of those that bother to communicate on Match.com fall off the face of the earth in less than 16 words

- 100% of those with motorcycles post a pic of them on the hog, therefore, I posted me on my sweet Vespa

If only half of these statements were true, I'd be thrilled. Enchanting, indeed.

Love,
S+

Biker Chick

COACHING NOTES: AUTHENTICITY

What is it about meeting people online that brings out deceit, dishonesty, and bizarre behavior? I know part of it is the lack of accountability, but why would anyone want to start a relationship based on lies? Age, weight, height, and marital status are common lies told to attract a person online. Once you actually meet the other person, three out of four of those factors are pretty obvious. Just what is the liar thinking?

I am fortunate never to have e-dated any e-liars or been harmed by any bizarre creeps. There are plenty of news reports of extreme cases that should serve to make you cautious. Use common sense when connecting in person. I usually had someone at my house when a date was picking me up and dropping me off, and always had a friend on standby when I was meeting someone out at a restaurant or other public place.

Early in my e-Harmony career, I was matched with a guy who answered the question, "What are three of your must-haves in life?" with:

1. sex
2. sex
3. sex

That was an easy match to close.

Another time, a match had an extensive description of one of his major hobbies, as running the website called "BigFootLivesInDowntownDallas.com." I am not making this up. Of course, I searched it and it totally freaked me out. He had pictures of the West End portion of downtown Dallas with areas circled where Big Foot was sighted. The journal entries that followed were incomprehensible, full of attempted poetry and what could have been his drug-trip diary. I reported him to eHarmony.

I'm your coach, not your mother, but please be careful out there.

WHAT A LITTLE TRIP TO PARIS CAN DO

Hi, Team,

Long time, no blog. Rock star Team member Angela took me along on a work trip to Geneva, Switzerland, since her hubby couldn't go. Although we purposely went to Switzerland, we ended up in Paris because of the volcano ash from Greenland in the air. April in Paris can do a lot toward making the heart grow fonder.

April in Paris is meant for love.

Big news! Nice Fella is *top and only* on the list. In fact, tonight, I turned off Match.com and eHarmony. The qualifier on how important that is might lie in the report on the previous blog about online dating. But really and truly, he is a gem and I am so enjoying getting to know him. Met his kids this week. This is the first time I have dated a guy with kids, and it is a new dynamic to explore.

Nice Fella has a strong and growing faith, is a committed, full-time dad, involved in a downtown homeless ministry, loves his church and serves there, has a job and all his own teeth. He is a great communicator and very purposeful about getting to know me. No tats to report.

Hats off to Curry!

Love,
S+

COACHING NOTES: COMMUNICATION IS KEY

Nice Fella wrote the book on relational communication. He is honest, funny, and intentional in the way he pursues our relationship. He never left me guessing as to what was next or where we stood. I was deeply honored to be on the receiving end of his care and genuinely appreciated his interpersonal style. I do not have this gift, so I am trying hard to learn and reciprocate. If you spend time with someone that cannot connect with you, share his or her heart, and understand yours, it might be a red flag and merit a deeper look.

TIME-OUT? TEAM BREAK? GAME OVER?

Hi, all,

Just to let you know, you are formally off the hook for a while, hopefully longer.

Nice Fella is worth it.

Love,
S+

COACHING NOTES: TIMING

Eternity is a long time, longer than we on earth can fathom. Yet, God operates in the eternity zone, and as a follower of Christ, I am asked to trust His goodness and timing. I waited for Mr. Sharla—and not always patiently. I pleaded, bargained, cried, and stomped my feet over the years, and God was unchanging in finding the best for me. You might struggle with His timing. Please know that when you cannot see his hand, trust his heart.

TIMING

There is a time for everything, and a season for every activity under the heavens:

a time to be born and a time to die,

a time to plant and a time to uproot,
a time to kill and a time to heal,
a time to tear down and a time to build,
a time to weep and a time to laugh,
a time to mourn and a time to dance,
a time to scatter stones and a time to gather them, a time to embrace and a time to refrain from embracing,
a time to search and a time to give up,
a time to keep and a time to throw away,
a time to tear and a time to mend, a time to be silent and a time to speak,
a time to love and a time to hate,
a time for war and a time for peace.

What do workers gain from their toil? I have seen the burden God has laid on the human race. He has made everything beautiful in its time. He has also set eternity in the human heart; yet no one can fathom what God has done from beginning to end.

Ecclesiastes 3:1–11 (NIV)

ELECTION DAY— I'M VOTING FOR NICE FELLA

Hi, Team,

It has been a long, wonderful weirdo break—and shall continue. So get comfortable and chill a while. In honor of Election Day 2010, just thought I'd cast my vote for Nice Fella. Some of you have had the pleasure of meeting him. I hope the rest of you do soon. We are spending Thanksgiving in Austin with his family and going to the UT Longhorns football game.

I'm extremely grateful for this man. He loves Jesus and he loves me.

I love you all!

S+

COACHING NOTES: IN-LAWS

In my dating career, there were a few guys whose families I liked more than the guy himself. There are plenty of jokes and horror stories about in-laws, but they are part of the deal. Might I suggest you decide up front to work hard and love unconditionally? There are plenty of resources to help you integrate into the new family and plenty of Psalms of anguish and joy. Remember, a lifetime is a long time.

I am blessed that Nice Fella comes from a nice family. Although I will not meet his mom until I get to heaven, her mark on the family is evident, and I am grateful.

STOP THE MADNESS

Hi, all,

It's been a while, but it is finally time to shut 'er down. This is the last entry for Team Sharla. The team is now retired. Touchdown, goal, home run, game-set-match…and any other winning term you can think of. I am going to officially be Mrs. Mark Langston.

Go, God. Amen!

Big thanks to the team for always being there—your support, friendship, love, advice, input, ear, and life!

Love,
S+

POST-GAME RESULTS

ENGAGEMENT

Easter morning is my favorite time of the year. Highland Park Presbyterian Church holds a sunrise worship service in the park where folks bring blankets and some—including me—wear their jammies. Two traditions I followed for this service were wearing my green with pink bonnets jammie pants and meeting friends Don and Sherry at Bubba's Diner for breakfast afterward.

Easter 2011 was Mark's first time to experience worship in the park and it was beautiful, reverent, and hope-filled. I did wear my fave jammie pants and we did go to Bubba's, but Mark added a new twist. After worship, as we strolled back to the car along the lake, we sat down on a park bench. We reflected on the service, its message, and our pleasure of worshipping together. At that moment, the world was as it should be. Here I was celebrating the resurrection of Christ with my sweetie and church family in a beautiful outdoor setting. I could have been in a beer commercial with, "it just doesn't get any better than this," except that it was 7 a.m., and I don't like beer. And then the world stopped, or at least it slowed down to warp speed minus five. He did it, went down on one knee, pulled out the ring, and asked me to spend the rest of my life with him. I cannot repeat the exact words, but they were romantic, mushy, idyllic, dreamy and overwhelming. I was a blubbering mess and I managed to say yes before we made our way to Bubba's to celebrate. Don and Sherry treated us with the best breakfast ever.

The following weekend, my dad fell and had a stroke while on his way to the gym. He was eighty-five and going strong, didn't take any prescription medications, still mowed the yard, and played a mean game of golf. It was a shock to us all to see him in ICU, intubated, and with a broken hip. That summer was spent traveling back and forth from Dallas to Shreveport, Louisiana, to see him in the hospital. Most wedding planning was done online, and I ordered my wedding dress while in the ICU waiting room.

My mom was worn thin from long hours and twice daily trips to the hospital as the therapists worked diligently to help my dad to walk, talk, and eat again. He was never able to do any of those basic skills, and four months later, he passed away. Two days before he died, Mark and I were able to have a wedding blessing performed in his room with my family. My dad was alert, and we felt he was fully aware of the significance of giving my hand to Mark. It was a bittersweet gift, and I cherish the memory.

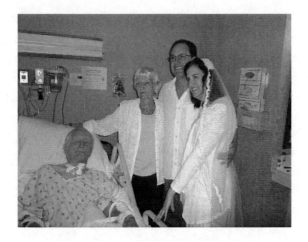

Wedding Blessing Ceremony

WEDDING HIGHLIGHTS

Guess what? When you marry at age fifty, there are no rules. Mark thought I would want the wedding before my fiftieth birthday in September. This is Texas and it is still raging hot in September, and there was no way I was sweating on my wedding day. The girls from The Best Small Group Ever each received an invitation *not* to serve as bridesmaids. Mark's son was his best man and his daughter was my best woman. The four Schulz boys ushered, each wearing a different colored polo shirt of the team colors for University of Texas and Louisiana State University. The mother of the bride wore pants, and we departed the wedding on my sweet Vespa—me in cowboy boots. At ages 50 and 52 and about to combine two households, we sure didn't need another toaster. We knew we wouldn't register for gifts, but wanted to honor the desire others might have to bless us. So, we opened a Giving Fund at the National Christian Foundation to allow others a chance to give to us, and then we were blessed to give it away. Each time we made a grant out of our fund, we had double the joy remembering the friends who contributed to the fund.

Wedding Escape

For years, brides have told me they really don't remember the wedding reception and didn't get to eat any food. Instead of a big dinner reception, we held a party the following night for out-of-town guests at the Cavanaugh air museum in a hangar full of restored World War II planes and vehicles. Mark and I rode inside a WWII tank and popped out to join the party. Sweet friends Terese and D'Ann decorated the hangar, and we all danced and ate until late.

I can't encourage you enough to buck tradition and do what makes sense and makes you happy while honoring the God who united you in marriage.

Tank Arrival

LIFE CONTINUES

For most of my twenties and thirties, I lived convinced that if I could just marry the guy for me, life would be so much better. I'm probably not alone in that misguided thought, as many of us live today wishing for something in the future. Whether it's a new job, a mate, a promotion, a new house, having a child, or another honorable desire, by setting our happy-factor on what we do not have, we miss out in the blessings God has for us today. The old saying, "Bloom where you are planted," carries a deep truth, and that is that God has something sweet for us exactly where we are.

And when God does bring you the desire of your heart, might I suggest you rejoice and batten down the hatches. From engagement through our second anniversary, our lives were in turmoil. I lost both my parents and a dear friend, turned fifty, left full-time employment, started a business, and suffered through menopause. Mark lost his dad and brother-in-law and changed jobs. We moved four times and purchased our first home together. I am grateful once again for God's timing in giving me a partner with whom to experience these hardships.

HAPPY ENDING

I am reminded daily of the struggles faced this side of heaven. All those years I struggled with singleness are slowly shrinking in the rearview mirror. It is an honor to encourage you to struggle well, struggle with grace, take God for his word, and when searching for a mate, search heavenward.

APPENDIX A
PRAYER LOG

I call on you, my God, for you will answer me;
turn your ear to me and hear my prayer.

(Psalm 17:6, NIV)

Date	Prayer Request	Answered Prayer

*By day the Lord directs his love, at night his song
is with me—a prayer to the God of my life.*

(Psalm 42:8, NIV)

Date	Prayer Request	Answered Prayer

May my prayer be set before you like incense;
may the lifting up of my hands be like the evening sacrifice.

(Psalm 141:2, NIV)

Date	Prayer Request	Answered Prayer

Lord, hear my prayer, listen to my cry for mercy;
in your faithfulness and righteousness come to my relief.

(Psalm 143:1, NIV)

Date   Prayer Request   Answered Prayer

_____

_____

_____

_____

_____

_____

_____

_____

_____

_____

_____

_____

_____

_____

_____

_____

_____

_____

APPENDIX B
TEAM ROSTER

*Perfume and incense bring joy to the heart, and the
pleasantness of a friend springs from their heartfelt advice.*

(Proverbs 27:9, NIV)

Name   Special Talent

_____

_____

_____

_____

_____

_____

_____

_____

_____

_____

_____

_____

One who loves a pure heart and who speaks with grace
will have the king for a friend.

(Proverbs 22:11, NIV)

Name   Special Talent

_____

_____

_____

_____

_____

_____

_____

_____

_____

_____

_____

_____

_____

_____

_____

_____

_____

_____

APPENDIX C
EXPOSURE AND ACTIVITY LOG

Diligent hands will rule, but laziness ends in forced labor.

(Proverbs 12:24, NIV)

Date	Exposure/Activity	Follow-up

A sluggard's appetite is never filled,
but the desires of the diligent are fully satisfied.

(Proverbs 13:4, NIV)

Date	Exposure/Activity	Follow-up

Be diligent in these matters; give yourself wholly
to them, so that everyone may see your progress.

(1 Timothy 4:15, NIV)

Date	Exposure/Activity	Follow-up

APPENDIX D
JOURNAL

Let love and faithfulness never leave you;
bind them around your neck,
write them on the tablet of your heart.

(Proverbs 3:3, NIV)

_____

_____

_____

_____

_____

_____

_____

_____

_____

_____

_____

_____

_____

_____

_____

_____

This is what the Lord, the God of Israel, says:
"Write in a book all the words I have spoken to you."

(Jeremiah 30:2, NIV)

_____

_____

_____

_____

_____

_____

_____

_____

_____

_____

_____

_____

_____

_____

_____

_____

_____

_____

_____

_____

_____

Write, therefore, what you have seen,
what is now and what will take place later.

(Revelation 1:19, NIV)

_____

_____

_____

_____

_____

_____

_____

_____

_____

_____

_____

_____

_____

_____

_____

_____

_____

_____

He who was seated on the throne said, "I am making everything new!" Then he said, "Write this down, for these words are trustworthy and true."

(Revelation 21:5, NIV)

_____

_____

_____

_____

_____

_____

_____

_____

_____

_____

_____

_____

_____

_____

_____

_____

_____

_____

APPENDIX E
TEAM GOODS

Ignite your team to pray and involve you in opportunities to meet new people with customized team goods they will wear and use with JOY. Pick from a unique selection of great practical items with fun color combinations and designs. In just a few clicks, you can have your team decked out and ready to play. Visit www.SharlaLangston.com to get your crowd sourced with brilliant and effective team goods.

Proceeds from your order will be given to Kingdom building ministries.

Track your orders and those who have received team goods here:

Item   Distributed to:

_____

_____

_____

_____

_____

_____

_____